DETECTIVE
RIDDLES

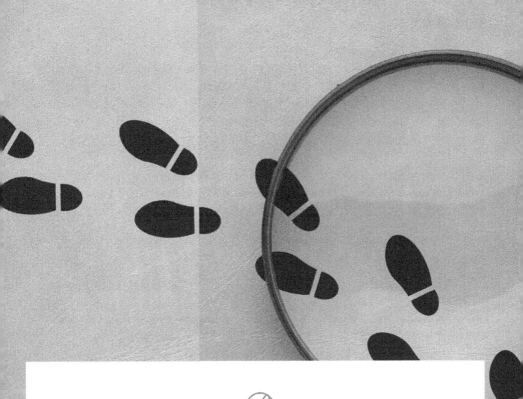

INTRODUCTION

When watching detective movies, you probably guess the criminals' names before the detectives do, exclaiming, "Come on, it's easy!" This is why the True Crime Publishing House team invites you to test your logic by solving these 65 puzzles. Learn right now whether you would have been a good detective!

I. The Murdering Type

Famous columnist Max Worthington was found deceased at his manual typewriter, fatally stabbed in the back. His agent, Roger, found his body when he went to check on Max to see why he hadn't submitted his latest column. He then called the police, and the dispatcher sent Detective Sing to investigate.

Detective Sing noticed that Max had apparently been writing his column when he was killed and that the last thing typed was "49t34 w5qgg3e j3," apparently a random string of numbers and letters created when his lifeless body slumped forward onto the typewriter.

Detective Sing questioned the people closest to Worthington and found several suspects: Max's ex-wife, Marisa, had been feuding with him over alimony payments she felt entitled to, despite his offer of the mansion they had shared, plus a generous lump-sum payment; Max's current girlfriend, Jillian, was a beautiful young woman but was seemingly high maintenance and seemed to miss his money more than him; and Max's brother, Gerald, was happy his brother was dead, as Max had stolen Marisa away from him, and Gerald was intent on winning her back.

Detective Sing concluded his investigation and quickly made an arrest - who did he take into custody?

2. 'Murder,' Quoth The Bible

Sean Donovin was found deceased in his hotel room bed at 3:15 PM on January 4 by the hotel maid. There were no apparent signs of foul play, and a cryptic note was left behind, so police initially assumed that Sean had taken his own life. However, a detective was called in just to be safe, and he immediately suspected foul play. Sean was a young man in his 20s, was engaged to be married, and was a successful businessman who also taught Sunday school. On the surface, he seemingly had no reason to commit such an act.

Since Sean passed in his hotel room and there was no sign of forced entry, the detective theorized that if he had been slain, it had to be one of the three people closest to him, as he didn't trust people easily. The three people closest to him were his sister, Hannah, who often assisted him with teaching Sunday school; his brother, John, who ran a small, semi-successful business; and, Sean's fiancee, Jenna.

Finding no obvious motive among the three, the detective held off on declaring Sean's end a suicide until after the medical examiner performed an autopsy. Sean had apparently perished from a lethal injection that killed him instantly. He was found approximately 11 hours after he passed. Still confounded by the evidence, the detective then began scouring the note for clues. It read:

"Jan 04/2009 4:10 AMMy loved ones, Jenna, Sis, John, I would just like to tell you how sorry I am. Blame God for why I am to die today. Blame Him. Seek Him if you want to know why I did leave you. Do not mourn my death. Please move on. Goodbye, Sean"

The detective found it strange that a seemingly pious and devout man would take his own life and then blaspheme against God, but the handwriting was verified to be Sean's.

After some thought, the detective deduced that Sean had been slain and arrested one of the three suspects. How did he know this, and who was the culprit?

3. Jumping To Conclusions

A body is found on the ground at the base of a multi-story building. The victim appears to have taken their own life by jumping out of one of the windows, but a detective is called to the scene nonetheless.

The detective enters the building, walks to the first-floor window immediately over the body, opens it, and tosses out a coin. He then goes to the second-floor window immediately over the body, opens it, and does the same.

He then proceeds to the window overlooking the body on each floor of the building, repeating the exact same procedure.

The gathered police think he's lost his mind, but once he has opened the window and tossed a coin from the top floor's window, he climbs back down to street level and tells the assembled police that the person was, in fact, murdered.

How did he deduce this?

4. Stone Cold Killer

The body of a hunter named Adrian was discovered at the bottom of a cliff, beneath the site where his girlfriend's dead body was found. He was still fully clothed in cold-weather apparel befitting of the season, including hiking boots, mittens, several layered jackets, and thick trousers made of wool.

A member of Adrian's hunting party named James was questioned, and he told the police that he had overheard Adrian having a heated argument with his girlfriend, Lulo. According to James, the argument became aggressive - Adrian picked up a rock and bashed Lulo over the head, killing her. After delivering the blow, Adrian looked up to see James watching him and was so startled that he turned and ran right off of the cliff to his demise.

James pointed out the rock that he believed Adrian had used to hit Lulo, and it was sent in for forensic analysis. After testing it, the lab discovered that Adrian's fingerprints were indeed on the rock that supposedly killed Lulo. The police immediately arrested James for Adrian's murder.

How did they conclude Adrian was slain and that James was the culprit when forensics seemed to corroborate James's story?

5. Sound The Alarm

Edward thought he had committed the perfect crime. He broke into a woman's house, strangled her in her bed, and staged the scene to look like an interrupted burglary. He ransacked the house, scattered the woman's possessions everywhere, and then smashed the patio door glass from the outside to stage a point of entry. Finally, he rigged the alarm and left to join his friends for a game of golf to establish an alibi.

Two hours later, while Edward was still walking the links, the alarm at the woman's house was triggered, and the police were alerted. When they arrived at the house, they found the scene just as Edward had staged it. There were no other people present, such as relatives or staff, and no animals that could have set off the alarm, which appeared to be functioning normally.

They concluded that the woman was indeed slain during a botched burglary.

One detective was suspicious of Edward, who was the woman's known enemy, but she couldn't figure out how he had rigged the alarm to go off hours after he left. How did he do it?

6. Special Delivery

A wealthy man was living alone in a small cottage. Partially disabled, he had many of life's necessities delivered to his home.

One Thursday afternoon, the mail carrier approached the cottage to deliver a letter and saw that the front door was left open. He peeked inside, only to find the wealthy man lying deceased on the floor in a pool of dried blood. The mailman immediately called the police, who investigated the scene for clues.

Even before inspecting the inside of the cottage, authorities made an arrest based on the items found on the porch, which included two bottles of milk, Monday's newspaper, a catalog, flyers, and several pieces of unopened mail.

Who was the culprit, and how did they know who did it based solely on the items on the porch?

7. Kidnapped Kid

A rich man's son was kidnapped. The ransom note told him to bring a valuable diamond to a phone booth in the middle of a public park.

Plainclothes police officers surrounded the park, intending to follow the criminal or his messenger. The rich man arrived at the phone booth and followed instructions but the police were powerless to prevent the diamond from leaving the park and reaching the crafty villain.

What did he do?

8. Self-Inflicted Gunshot Wound

John Aiers, a little person, was found dead in his living room from an apparent self-inflicted gunshot wound, the pistol still clutched in his lifeless hand.

There was no sign of a struggle and no indication of foul play - only the small bullet hole below his left breast and a small bloodstain around the wound. The bullet had gone clear through his body, through the couch he was sitting on, and had lodged in the wall behind him.

A junior detective surmised from the scene that Aiers had taken his own life, bolstered by the man's massive amount of financial debt and history of depression. However, the senior detective stated that he knew Aiers had been murdered the second he laid eyes on his body.

What did he notice that the junior detective had not?

9. Mystery of the Ancient Temple

Once upon a time there existed a temple in India which housed three identical idols which spoke to the devotees.

The idols were of - God of Truth, which always spoke the truth; God of Falsehood, which always lied; and God of Diplomacy which sometimes spoke the truth and at other times lied.

The pilgrims come from all parts of the world to get their questions answered by the Gods. But there was a problem. As the idols were indistinguishable, devotees were not sure from which idol to ask their questions and in turn they did not know which God has answered and whether to believe it or not.

Once a wise man visited the temple. He asked the question:

"Which God is seated at the centre?" to all the three idols.

The idol on the left, centre and right replied God of Truth, God of Diplomacy and God of Falsehood respectively.

The wise man at once proclaimed that he had solved the mystery of the temple.

10. Detective Bethoven

Handel has been killed and Beethoven is on the case.

He has interviewed the four suspects and their statements are shown below. Each suspect has said two sentences. One sentence of each suspect is a lie and one sentence is the truth.

Help Beethoven figure out who the killer is.

Joplin: I did not kill Handel. Either Grieg is the killer or none of us is.

Grieg: I did not kill Handel. Gershwin is the killer.

Strauss: I did not kill Handel. Grieg is lying when he says Gershwin is the killer.

Gershwin: I did not kill Handel. If Joplin did not kill him, then Grieg did.

Who is the killer?

II. Window Pain In The Neck

A man who arrives at his friend's house for a visit grows concerned when there's no answer at the door. Fearing the worst, he brushes the frost off of one of the window panes and looks inside to see his friend's lifeless body on the floor, his neck contorted in an unnatural manner.

The man calls the police, who quickly respond and enter the house to find the homeowner deceased, apparently of a broken neck.

The police ask the man to explain exactly what he was doing there and how he found his friend. The man reiterates that he was simply dropping by for a visit and decided to wipe the frost off of one of the window panes to peer inside when his friend didn't answer. Before he can finish, the police put the man in cuffs and arrest him for the murder of his friend.

How did they know he was lying?

12. Love At First Funeral

A young woman meets a mysterious young stranger at her mother's funeral. They hit it off immediately, but he leaves before she can get his personal information.

She can't stop thinking about the young man, but try as she might, she can't seem to find anyone who knows him and has no way of contacting him.

A few days later, her sister comes over to visit, and she, too, is unable to identify the man. The young woman always got along well with her sister, and they rarely fought, but she decides right then and there to kill her in such a way that no one will suspect she did it.

What went wrong? Why did the young woman hatch such a devious plan against a sister she always loved?

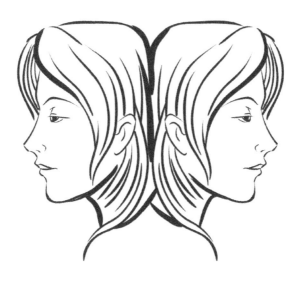

13. The Cook, The Maid, Two Friends, And A Niece

Wealthy bachelor Steven Andrews was murdered in his mansion overlooking the ocean. When Detective Carrie Marshall arrived on the scene around mid-afternoon, the local Riverside police had assembled the five suspects in front of a large bay window, each of whom had spent the night in the mansion: his cook, his maid, two of his friends, and his niece. Detective Marshall's partner, Lieutenant Linda Newton, who had arrived an hour earlier, shared that all of the suspects agreed that Steven had been alive a few minutes after midnight when they last saw him. Furthermore, none of them heard anything to indicate a murder had taken place before he was found at 6:30 AM by his niece, Mandy Andrews, when she had come downstairs to get a glass of water. She stated that she had seen her uncle's body near the bay window on her way back upstairs.

While Lieutenant Newton and the Riverside officers searched the house for clues, Detective Marshall interrogated the suspects, trying her best not to be distracted by the beautiful view of the sun setting over the ocean from the bay window.

The maid stated that she cleaned the dining room where Andrews had been entertaining his guests and then helped the cook put away the leftovers before retiring to her room shortly after 11:00 PM. She read in bed until approximately 12:30 AM and heard talking and laughter, but was unable to make out any conversations. Later that morning, she heard Mandy scream and rushed downstairs with the cook and Andrews's house guests to find the host's body lying in front of the bay window, dead from an apparent gunshot to the head.

The cook corroborated the maid's story, stating that she had tidied up the dining room and then helped him store the leftover food. He claimed that he went to his bedroom at the same approximate time that the maid had and that he had gone to sleep at approximately 11:30 PM after showering and brushing his teeth. He awoke when he heard a scream and rushed downstairs with the maid and the two house guests to find Andrews's lifeless body in front of the bay window.

Mandy stated that she was up until midnight with her uncle and his friends and then retired to her room, where she fell asleep at approximately 1:15 AM. She claimed that she woke up at precisely 6:24 AM and went downstairs to the kitchen for a glass of water. While pausing to admire the sunrise through the bay window on her way back upstairs, she noticed her uncle's body and screamed, alerting the others in the house. Without having to interrogate Andrews's two friends, Detective Marshall stated that she had solved the case. What had she learned that pointed to the culprit?

14. Share And Share Alike

A young woman is invited to the home of an older woman she had met earlier at a local farmer's market.

They chat briefly, but the young woman starts to feel uncomfortable and decides she had better get going.

The older woman acts offended and suggests that the young woman stay for just a bit longer to try one of the plump, juicy apples she had purchased at the farmer's market. Again, the young woman refuses, but the older woman insists, picking up a sharp kitchen knife and suggesting that they share the apple.

Intimidated by the knife, the young woman agrees. The older woman cuts the apple in half, and they each eat from their half of the apple. The old woman, who in actuality was a crazed serial killer, chomps on her half of the apple in delight as the young woman drops to the floor, dead.

How did the old woman kill the young woman?

15. Press Play For Murder

Police are called to the scene of an apparent suicide. When they arrive, they find a man deceased from a gunshot wound. He holds a pistol in one hand and an analog cassette recorder in the other. A detective arrives on the scene and presses "play" on the recorder. A man's voice says, "I have nothing else to live for. I can't go on."

Immediately after the last word, the recorder captures the sound of a single gunshot and then stops recording.The detective tells the assembled police to cordon off the area and wait for the forensics team, because the man did not take his own life - he was murdered.

How did the detective know this simply from listening to the recording?

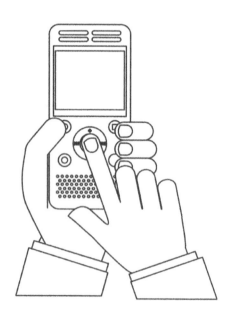

16. Message In The Sand

A detective is called to the site of a murder. A young woman who worked as a waitress at a nearby club called Jake's Palace had been hit over the head and then choked with a belt. Her attacker, assuming she was deceased, had left her there, but she had only been unconscious.

She managed to drag herself 20 feet toward's the water's edge, where she scrawled a message in the sand before passing from her head wound. The two officers who were first on the scene found two partially eroded letters that looked like an "h" and a "p" and assumed the victim had written "help" in the sand before the water began to wash them away.

While the detective is still assessing the scene, additional officers arrive, bringing three male suspects:
1) A man in ill-fitting clothing named Jersey who claimed he had only purchased the woman a drink at the club before she left without saying a word;
2) An older man named Shelby who owned Jake's Palace and claimed that he had seen the woman leave the club with the third man; and
3) A man who claimed the woman had only accompanied him to his car to get cigarettes and then returned to the club.

After listening to their stories, the detective believes he has enough to solve the case.

Who did it, and how did he know?

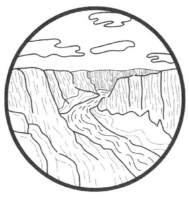

17. No Alibis In Murder Mansion

A millionaire was found slain in his mansion one Sunday morning in April. His wife, who discovered his body, immediately called the police, and an investigation commenced.

Detectives found that four people were present in the mansion or on the grounds at the time of the murder: the millionaire's wife, the cook, the maid, the gardener, and the butler.

All claimed to be innocent, yet none of them had an alibi, as they were all alone and in different areas when the act must have taken place: The millionaire's wife claimed that she had been reading a book; the maid claimed she was getting the mail; the gardener claimed that he was out on the grounds planting seeds; and the butler claimed that he had been busy polishing the silver.

After hearing their stories, the detectives immediately arrested one of the suspects and charged them with the millionaire's murder - but which one?

18. Loose lips

A man rushes into his wife's hospital room shouting, "Who shot her? Who shot my wife?" A police detective asks the man to calm down and explain himself. The man states that he is the woman's husband, and he demands justice for his wife.

The detective asks the man how he knew about his wife's condition, and the man says that he spent the night at a friend's house and called home in the morning to check on her. Their maid answered the phone and told him that his wife had been hurt and was at the hospital, and he immediately rushed there to see her.

He criticized the detective for standing around questioning him instead of looking for his wife's shooter. The detective smiled and told him that he didn't need to look for the shooter because he had found him. He then arrested the husband for attempted murder.

How did he know the husband was guilty?

19. Who Killed Maya?

Last night there was a Christmas party at the bar 'Snowman'. By 2 pm all the alcohol had been finished and the visitors began to drift away.

A group of friends said goodbye to Maya when she left. That was the last time anyone ever saw her. Her body has been found near the bar this morning.

The police arrived at the crime scene. After examining the body, the detective interviewed three suspects: Ryan, Kylie, and Jack.

Ryan said: When she left, I went to the bathroom.

Kylie said: I ordered one more beer at the bar.

Jack said: I was talking to the girl, I had just met.

Who killed Maya?

20. Who Is Lying?

Jane was found in her house lying in the center of a pentagram.

The police questioned three people they found in her recent calls.

Jane's brother: I have called her in the morning. She was depressed because she had been fired.

Jane's Neighbor: She borrowed a pretty sum of money from me and called to ask for more time.

Jane's Boss: She didn't show up to work for a few days.

I have called her to ask if anything happened.Who is lying?

21. Who Killed His Wife?

Katie was robbed and killed by her neighbor. He came to her house, took all her valuables and money, and decided to get rid of Katie so that she wouldn't rat him out.

Killer: Write a suicide note!

She writes: MY DEAR, FORGIVE ME! I LOVE YOU SO MUCH. HERE IS THE CODE OF OUR LOCKER IN THE BANK 73 63 22 32 73 81 PLEASE, CALL MY MOM.

And then the killer shoots her. After that, her husband reached the house and called the police. Husband read the note and says: So weird, we have no locker...Police say: There are no signs of a break-in. This must be one of your friends or neighbors. Do you suspect anyone?

Husband says: We have three suspicious neighbors. Peter, Drake, and Robert.

Police say: I will question them.

Peter: I have just returned from a business trip. Such horrible news!

Drake: I am shocked! at that time I was at mom's.

Robert: So sorry for Katie. Today I was out at the county fair.

Katie's husband was going to call her mom. He looked at the note again and suddenly realized who the murderer was.

Who killed his wife?

22. The Stolen Bracelet

A woman named Cathy goes to the police claiming that someone broke into her house and stole her diamond bracelet while she was at work.

The policemen investigate the crime scene and notice that the bedroom window is broken. There are muddy footprints all across the bedroom floor. However, the room is otherwise neat and organized. The following day, Cathy is arrested for fraud.

Can you figure out why?

23. The Old Woman Who Lived Alone

An elderly woman lived alone in her house by the suburbs. She rarely left the house and knew only a few people.

One Friday morning, the mailman called out for the woman but didn't receive a prompt answer as usual. Upon peeking in through the window, the mailman realized that the woman was murdered.

The police investigated the house and found Tuesday's newspaper by the dead body. Also, by the door outside, there were three unopened bottles of milk, one of which had gone bad.

The police arrested the killer the very next day.

How did they figure out so quickly?

24. Deadly Chemicals

A renowned chemist is found dead in his lab. There is no clear evidence except a piece of paper lying by the body. The paper is blank other than the name of five elements scrawled across it hastily:

- Nickel
- Carbon
- Oxygen
- Lanthanum
- Sulfur

The guard reported that three people visited the chemist that day - his sister, Lanaya, his colleague, Nicolas, and his wife, Teresa. The criminal was arrested immediately.

Who was it?

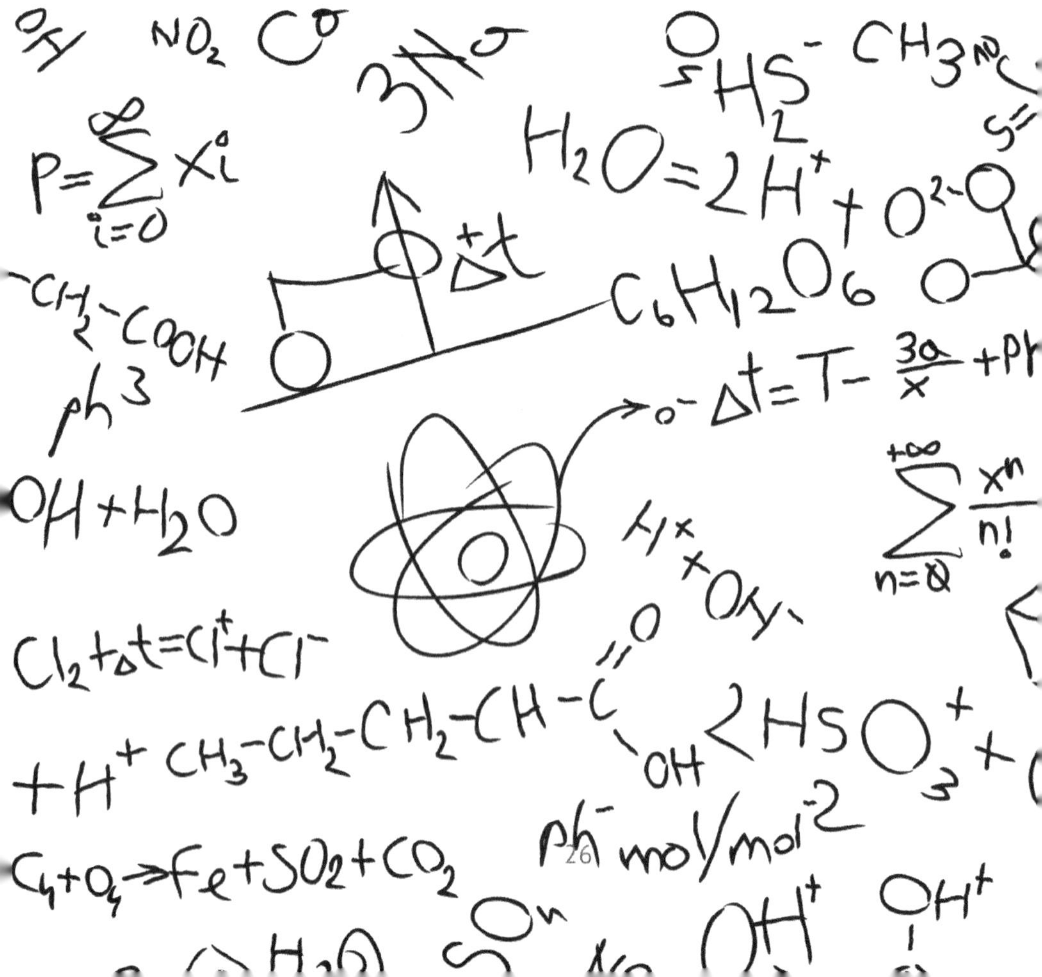

OH NO_2 CO $3N_2$

$P = \sum_{i=0}^{\infty} x_i$ $H_2O = 2H^+ + O^{2-}$ $O=\overset{-}{S}H_2^-$ CH_3

$^-CH_2-COOH$ $C_6H_{12}O_6$

ph^3 $\circ^- \Delta t = T - \frac{3a}{x} + Ph$

$OH + H_2O$ $\sum_{n=0}^{+\infty} \frac{x^n}{n!}$

$Cl_2 + \Delta t = Cl^+ + Cl^-$ $H^+ + OH^-$

$+H^+ \ CH_3-CH_2-CH_2-CH-CH-C \overset{O}{\underset{OH}{<}} \ 2HSO_3^+ +$

$C_4 + O_2 \rightarrow Fe + SO_2 + CO_2$ ph^- mol/mol^2

OH^+ OH^+

25. Grand Theft Auto

A car thief, who had managed to evade the authorities in the past, unknowingly took the automobile that belonged to Detective Thompson. The sleuth wasted no time and spared no effort in discovering and carefully examining the available clues. He was able to identify four suspects with certainty that one of them was the culprit.

The four make the statements below. From twelve of total statements, six are true and six false.

Suspect A:
1. C and I have met many times before today.
2. B is guilty.
3. The car thief did not know it was the Detective's car.

Suspect B
:1. D did not do it.
2. D's third statement is false.
3. I am innocent.

Suspect C:
1. I have never met A before today.
2. B is not guilty.
3. D knows how to drive.

Suspect D:
1. B's first statement is false.
2. I do not know how to drive.
3. A did it.

Which one is the car thief?

26. The Poison Murderer

On a hot summer day Detective Thompson finds a man dead in a room locked from the inside. After an autopsy, he was proved to be killed by poison.

In the locked room, there was a cup of cola and a half cup of water. After examination of the beverages, the cola contained 20% poison, and the cup of water contained 100% poison.

It was evident that someone had sneaked into his room before he came back from work and put the poison.

Detective Thompson hasn't found the killer yet, but he already figured it out where the murderer put the poison.

Where is it?

27. Job Interview

Detective Thompson decided to hire a new assistant. He had three candidates and he decided to give them a quiz.

He said, "Look Guys, there's a crime that needs to be solved and there's a clue in one of the public libraries in Brooklyn. The clue is stuck inside a book, between pages 165 and 166.

Two of the guys jumped up and bolted out the door. The third guy just sat there. Detective Thompson said to the man who remained, "You got the job."

Why did he get the job?

28. The Diamond Robbery

Detective Thompson knocked on Mr. Fred's door. It was a case of robbery. Mr.Fred's diamond has been stolen. The thief was very intelligent. He first disabled Mr. Fred's safety device and then stole the diamond. The thief also didn't leave any fingerprint.

When Detective Thompson questioned Mr. Fred, he said that he had been sound asleep when the incident happened, and he did not know at what time the diamond was stolen.

Detective Thompson then went out to question the keeper, the only other person living with Mr. Fred at that time. The keeper said that he had been to his mother's place and did not have any information on the incident.

Then Detective Thompson walked around outside the house to see if he could get any more clues. Walking on pieces of the glass, he saw that the window was broken. After a closer examination he saw that the window had been broken with the help of a hammer.

After some time, Detective Thompson decided to arrest Mr. Fred for faking robbery.

How did he knew that Mr. Fred had a part to play in this crime?

29. Archeological Dig

"I've finally earned my place as assistant curator of the museum", said Bob to his friend, Detective Thompson.

"I moved West of the Pakistani dig site and we've just unearthed some wonderful coin artifacts."

"Why did you start digging in a new location?" asked Detective Thompson.

"One of the local natives told me that, for many generations, his family had passed down a legend of a lost village and he found a map among his father's things," said Bob.

"His father recently passed away", he added.

"The native followed the map and led me to this site on the condition that if we discovered anything of value he would be paid one thousand dollars", explained Bob.

"And what is it that you found buried,?" asked Detective Thompson.

"It's just terrific," exclaimed Bob,

"we found 3 gold coins of various sizes dated 400 B.C., and after properly dusting them off I found them to be in excellent condition."

"I quickly paid the native to complete our verbal contract and keep him from trying to claim a portion of the discovery," concluded Bob.

After considering for a few moments, Detective Thompson suggested Bob that when he returns home he should look for another job!

How come?

30. The Burglary Job

A man was gunned down in his flat by a burglar, who then ransacked the flat. The case was placed in the capable hands of Inspector Baldwin of Scotland Yard.

Baldwin's investigation revealed that one man had planned the crime, another had carried it out, and a third had acted as lookout and fourth one was somehow present unaware of plan. Baldwin discussed the case over lunch with an old friend, Detective Thompson.

"It's quite a case," Thompson remarked. "Any suspects?"

"Yes indeed. Four. We have conclusive evidence that three of those four were responsible for the crime," said Baldwin. "The fourth had no prior knowledge of the crime and is completely innocent. The problem is that we're not sure which of the four are the planner, the gunman, the lookout, and the innocent bystander," he added.

"I see." said Thompson while drinking his tea. "What do you know about them at this point?"

"Well, the names of the four are Erick, Joss, Hewitt, and Cooper. Cooper and Joss play tennis together every Saturday. They're an odd pair! Cooper can't drive, and Joss has been out of Prison for only a year," Baldwin answered.

"We know that Erick and Cooper kept the flat under the surveillance for several days just before the day the crime was committed, the 17th. Hewitt and Erick, with their wives, had dinner together on the 12th."

"We also know that the gunman spent the week before the crime in Edinburgh, and that the innocent bystander was acquainted with the planner and the gunman, but not with the lookout."

"That's very helpful," said Thompson with a smile. "Baldwin, your case is complete!"

Who were the gunner, the planner, the lookout, and the bystander?

31. The Dying Message

During his vacation in a small lakeside village, once again Detective Thompson must faced with a homicide case. This time, Mrs. Bennet, a local middle-age woman that was also a widow of rich businessman was found stabbed in the chest at her bedroom. Knowing Thompson reputation, local Inspector Lucas lets him examine the crime scene.

"It seems that Mrs. Bennet is familiar with the murderer, as there was no sign of struggle. The bedroom's door is locked from the inside. The possibility is that she was stabbed right in front of the door, probably when she opened the door for the killer. She then still managed to slam the door and locked it." explained the Inspector.

"She didn't die instantly, and still managed to crawl halfway to her study desk, probably looking for a pen to wrote the killer's name. Unfortunately, she didn't make it and die right next to her bed," Isnpector Lucas added.

The Inspector looked hesitate for a moment before continue with his story, "As you can see on the bed there are some gift-wrapping paper in various color. It seems that Mrs. Bennet was wrapping some boxes before the incident. When we found her body, Mrs. Bennet right hand was grasping a yellow and blue pieces of papers. I don't know whether it means something or not, or probably she wanted to write the killer's name with blood on the paper using her left hand.

"One thing for sure, all witnesses has agreed that all doors in the house are locked at the moment of the incident, which leave four suspects that happened to be inside the home that time:

- Ana Lucia, a maid that has been working for a year for Mrs. Bennet. She was the first to notice something wrong when Mrs. Bennet didn't answer when she knocked the door to bringing Mrs. Bennet lunch to the bedroom.

- Dr. Robert Green, Mrs. Bennet personal doctor, and rumor said it that they have an affair. The doctor said that approximately ten minutes before Ana Lucia delivered the lunch, he went to Mrs. Bennet's bedroom for their medical appointment. She didn't open the door and told the doctor to wait for a while, as she was busy.

- Alan Bennet, son of the late Mr. Bennet, and Mrs' Bennet stepson. He was watching television in his room when Ana Lucia called. He and Dr. Green then broke in to Mrs. Bennet's room to found her lying dead on the floor. Alan then phoned the police and ambulance while the doctor checked Mrs. Bennet.

- Tony Forrester, a friend of Alan Bennet. He didn't acquainted with Mrs. Bennet. He was already in the bathroom for 15 minutes before the incident, as he admitted that he was having a constipation during that time.

"So, what do you think detective? Apparently, all four suspects don't have a strong alibi," asked Inspector Lucas to Detective Thompson.

"Hmmm... yes it's true that there's no strong evidence that points to the killer. But there's an obvious clue and you should focus your interrogation to one person," Thompson answered.

Who is the strong suspect, and what is the clue?

32. Are You Mocking Me?

One snowy night, Detective Thompson was in his house reading a book while sitting by a fire. All of a sudden a snowball came crashing through his window, breaking it. Thompson got up and looked out the window just in time to see three neighborhood brats who were brothers run around a corner.

Their names were Alan Jones, Mark Jones and Peter Jones.

Underestimate Thompson reputation as a cunning detective, the two innocent brats teased him by sent a note with clue on Thompson front door.

The note reads "? Jones. He broke your window."

Which one of the three Jones brothers should Thompson question about the incident?

33. Thompson's Game

Detective Thompson's nephew is gonna have a birthday party, and he's being asked to hold a logic game where the winner will get a prize.

At the party, Thompson took two large bowls, one wood and one plastic, and placed them up high so that the kids couldn't see the contents. He then said, "One is filled with a valuable prize, while the other is empty. You get whatever is in the bowl you pick. You can pick only once, but you must decipher my clues and explain to me which bowl you think has the prize and why. And no random guessing allowed."

He then gave them these clues:

1. The polyester shirt I'm wearing.

2. A cotton shirt in my closet.

3. A hollow cardboard toilet paper roll.

4. This plastic cup I'm drinking my tea from.

5. The acrylic socks I'm wearing.

6. An empty paper lunch bag.

All the kids were stumped for quite some time. Thompson started to wonder whether his puzzle was too hard for kids, until one young girl gave him the correct answer. What do the clues have in common with each other that show the prize bowl?

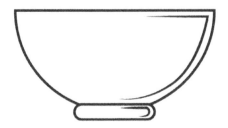
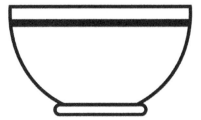

34. Diamonds Are Forever

Detective Thompson attended a call from the millionaire Mr. Bronson. He entered the closed display room of the magnificent Mr. Bronson's house.

With a quick sweep of his eyes, Thompson noted that the room was round (no corners).

- To the left there was a waiter, next to him a little beverage table with 5 glasses filled with chopped ice and some bottles.

- To the center there was a little table with a small open chest (Obviously something was missing).

- To the right there was Mrs Rochelle in front of a Renoir painting, then there was Mr. Potter in front of a Picasso, and then Mr. Reiss, in front of a Rembrandt. Mr. Bronson stands beside Mr. Reiss.No more person, furniture, nor appliances than those were in the room.

Mr. Bronson explained: "Detective Thompson, I entered my guest to show them my treasures. First I showed them the beautiful collection of diamonds that were in the chest on that table, and are now missing. And then each one of us went to admire my paintings."

"My guests are standing right where they were at the time I discovered the disappearance. As you can see, we all gave our backs to the diamond's table to see the pictures. And everyone was admiring the works so attentively, that no one paid attention to the others. Then I turned back and the diamonds were gone," Bronson added.

Detective Thompson asked about the waiter. "I called him for some refreshment. He was serving the glasses, we all heard him chopping the ice. I personally searched him. He doesn't have the diamonds," Mr. Bronson answered. "I cannot search my guests, as it would be an insult. Nobody has left the room. And there's no place to hide the stones!," he added.

Detective Thompson calmed down the poor Mr. Bronson and then solved the crime easily.

Who is the theft, and where he/she hid the diamonds?

35. Weak Hand

Detective Thompson came from America to visit an acquaintance in England, and he stayed at his friend's mansion. Besides Thompson and his host, there are four more persons invited, one fellow American named Alex, and other three British man, Ian, John, and Davie.

Over a dinner of fine English cuisine, the group discussed the differences between the two countries. As is often the case when a bunch of guys get together, the topic turned to sports. The Americans, especially Alex, bragged about baseball and how he used to play, and the British lads told about the history of cricket.

As the night wore on, one of the British businessman, Ian, realized he wanted to get a report he had left in his office. He excused himself to retrieve it. Thompson who were bored then asked if he could ride along with him.

They were gone only a short time, but when they returned to the mansion they were surprised to see police cars parked in front. An officer approached the two men, asked them to identify themselves, and explained that a servant had been attacked. The host, Ian, and Thompson were cleared of charge, meaning that one of the other three guests (Alex, John, Davie) was the attacker.

The servant had been stabbed in the front right shoulder, and had managed to call the police before he passed out. An ambulance took the servant to hospital, and, needless to say, the police were eager to solve the crime. They weren't sure if the servant was going to survive to identify the attacker.

Ian explained that he had an idea how to find out who did it. He assembled all the men in the study, and began strutting in front of the fireplace, talking in a quite animated manner about what he thought had happened, didn't realized that there was a real detective present.

Near the fevered climax of his presentation, Ian picked up three trinkets from the mantelpiece, and tossed them one by one to the three suspects, who in turn caught them with one hand.

Ian had concluded that, since the servant's wounds were in the front right shoulder, the attacker was left-handed, and the person who caught the trinket in his left hand was the culprit.

Alex and John managed to catch it, while Davie dropped the trinket. But to his dismay, each of the three men tried to catch the trinket with his right hand.

A bored looking policeman said, "Well, it doesn't look like that worked."

"Just then, Detective Thompson stood up and said, "Actually, Ian's trick worked quite well. And I have to say I'm sorry that I was my fellow countryman Alex who did it."

How did Thompson know?

36. Royal Riddle

An Emperor of ancient Asian kingdom is looking for a wife that also can serve as grand advisor. He then summons three most beautiful women in his region, and now will decide who's the wisest among them. After passing many tests of wit, cunning, and invention, they were pitted against each other in a decisive final battle.

Led blind-folded into a small room, the three smart women were seated around a small wooden table as the Emperor described the test for them.

"Upon each of your heads I have placed a hat. Now you are either wearing a blue hat or a white hat. All I will tell you is this-at least one of you is wearing a blue hat. There may be only one blue hat and two white hats, there may be two blue hats and one white hat, or there may be three blue hats. But you may be certain that there are not three white hats."

"I will shortly remove your blind folds, and the test will begin. The first to correctly announce the color of his hat shall be my wife and this kingdom grand advisor. Be warned however, she who guesses wrongly shall be beheaded. If not one of you answers within the hour, you will be sent home and I will seek elsewhere for wisdom."

With that, the Emperor uncovered the women' eyes and sat in the corner and waited. One woman looked around and saw that her competitors each were wearing blue hats. From the look in their eyes she could see their thoughts were the same as hers, "What is the color of my hat?"

For what seemed like hours no one spoke.

Finally she stood up and said, "The color of the hat I am wearing is..."

37. One Wish

Once upon a time, in the Kingdom of Atreus, a king lives with his loyal servant.

After service of about 40 years, the king became ill and was going to die. One day, the king called his servant and asked him for a wish. It could be any wish but just one. The king gave him one day to think about it.

The servant became very happy and went to his mother for discussion about the wish.

His mother was blind and she asked her son for making a wish for her eye-sight to come back. Then the servant went to his wife.

She became very excited and asked for a son as they were childless for many years.

After that, the servant went to his father who wanted to be rich and so he asked his son to wish for a lot of money.

The next day, the servant went to the king and made one wish through which all the three (mother, father, wife) got what they wanted.

What's the servant wish?

38. Sports Day

During the recent school sports day, four girls were competing in the 200 meters sprint.

The race was won by Janet, but the rest of them finished on a close call. Official figures mysteriously went missing just after the event, so it was kinda hard to decide to whom the silver and bronze medal had to be given.

However, various spectators could remember the following information:

1. Janet won and wore red.

2. The girl wearing number 1 came third.

3. Julie beat the girl in yellow, but wasn't wearing number 2.

4. Only one girl finished in the same position as the number she wore, but she didn't wear red.

5. Jessica beat the girl wearing number 3 and Josie wore yellow.

6. The girl in green wore number 2.

7. A spectator remembered one girl wore blue, but couldn't remember anything else about her.

Can you determine the positions the girls finished in, along with the numbers and colors they wore?

39. Adventure Race

There are four people in an adventure race that need to get across a lake. They have only one small canoe.

The rules say that only the slowest person in the canoe can paddle, only one or two can be in the canoe at a time, and they must all cross in the canoe.

From practice, they know that:

- Annie can paddle across in 1 minute.

- Bob can paddle across in 2 minutes.

- Charles can paddle across in 5 minutes.

- Dan can paddle across in 10 minutes.

How do they get everyone across the river in 17 minutes without breaking the rules?

40. Pennies

There are three clay containers. One of them has only pennies from the year 2005 in it, one has only pennies from the year 1975 in it, and the third has an equal number of each.

They are labeled "2005," "1975" and "MIXED".

However, you know that the labels have been switched, so that NONE of the container is marked correctly.

Can you properly label the containers without looking in them, and ONLY pulling ONE coin out from ONE container?

41. Bulbs

There are three switches downstairs.

Each corresponds to one of the three light bulbs in the attic.

You can turn the switches on and off and leave them in any position.

How would you identify which switch corresponds to which light bulb, if you are only allowed ONE trip upstairs?

42. Farmer's Dilemma

An old farmer went on a trip with a fox, a goose and a sack of corn.

He came upon a river which he had to cross and found a tiny boat to use to cross the stream.

He could only take himself and one other - the fox, the goose, or the corn - at a time.

He could not leave the fox alone with the goose or the goose alone with the corn.

How he can cross all of them safely?

43. Great Pumpkin

So, you've angered the spirit of Halloween by failing to revere the Great Pumpkin, and now a curse has befallen you. On the walkway home, you find a Ward of Seven Jack O' Lanterns arranged in a circle.

If midnight comes and any of the seven are still lit, a dark reaper and seven dark horses with seven dark riders shall visit thy abode. They shall surround thy domicile and, while circling it, they will proceed to pelt thy dwelling with eggs and cream of shaving. And come morn there will be a great mess to be reckoned with. So you better get those lanterns out.

Unfortunately, you quickly discover something odd about these lanterns. When you blow out the first one, the lanterns on either side extinguish as well! But there is more. If you blow out a lantern adjacent to one that is extinguished, the extinguished one(s) will relight.

It seems that blowing on any lantern will change the state of three - the one you blew on and its two neighbors.

Finally, you can blow on an extinguished lantern and it will relight, and its neighbors will light/extinguish as applicable.

Frightened by the sound of many hooves, you try to clear your mind and solve this puzzle....

44. Smart Farmer

A poor but smart farmer is convicted for fraud against rich governor.

He gets the death penalty for his crime.

The judge allows him to say a last sentence in order to determine the way the penalty will be carried out.

If the farmer lies, he will be hanged, if he speaks the truth he will be beheaded.

The farmer speaks a last sentence and to everybody surprise some minutes later he is set free because the judge cannot determine his penalty.

What did the farmer say?

45. Point To The Murderer

There are five people.

One of them shot and killed one of the other five.

We know following clues:

1. Dan ran in the NY City Marathon yesterday with one of the innocent men.

2. Mike consider being a farmer before he moved to the city.

3. Jeff is a top notch computer consultant and wants to install Ben new computer next week.

4. The murderer had his leg amputated last month.

5. Ben met Jack for the first time six months ago.

6. Jack has been in seclusion since the crime.

7. Dan used to drink heavily.

8. Ben and Jeff built their last computers together.

9. The murderer is Jack brother. They grew up together in Seattle.

Consider yourself to be a famous detective "Sherlock Homles", can you find the killer?

46. Detective Tip

Sherlock, A detective who was mere days from cracking an international smuggling ring has suddenly gone missing. While inspecting his last-known location, you find a note:

710 57735 34 5508 51 7718

Currently, there are 3 suspects: Bill, John, and Todd.

Can you break the detective's code and find the criminal's name?

47. Who Is The Killer?

Tarun Asthaniya is found dead in his office at his desk. The police have narrowed the suspects down to three people: Mrs. Harish Kumar, Taruns wife Himanshi Asthaniya and his buisness partner Mr. Jason Negi.

All three visited Tarun on the day of his murder, but all three provide the police with stories of explanation as to the reason for their visit.

Police found Mr. tarun with his wrist watch still on his right arm, a torn up picture of his wife laying on the floor beside the trash can, and an ink pen in his right hand.

On the desk, the police found a name plate, a telephone that was off the hook, and a personal calendar turned to the July 5th page with 7B91011 written on it. After examining this evidence, the police knew their suspect.

Who was it ?

48. Murder Mystery Problem

One evening there was a murder in the home of married couple, their son and daughter. One of these four people murdered one of the others.

One of the members of the family witnessed the crime.

The other one helped the murderer.

These are the things we know for sure:

1. The witness and the one who helped the murderer were not of the same sex.

2. The oldest person and the witness were not of the same sex.

3. The youngest person and the victim were not of the same sex.

4. The one who helped the murderer was older than the victim.

5. The father was the oldest member of the family.

6. The murderer was not the youngest member of the family.

Who was the murderer?

49. Elevator Puzzle

A man who lives on the tenth floor takes the elevator down to the first floor every morning and goes to work.

In the evening, when he comes back; on a rainy day, or if there are other people in the elevator, he goes to his floor directly. Otherwise, he goes to the seventh floor and walks up three flights of stairs to his apartment.

Can you explain why?

50. Crack The Code

During a secret mission, an agent gave the following code to the higher authorities

AIM DUE OAT TIE MOD

However the information is in one word only and the rest are fake. To assist the authorities in understanding better, he also sent them a clue - If I tell you any one character of the code, you can easily find out the number of vowels in the code word.

Can you find out the code word?

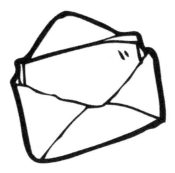

51. Point To The Thief

A Japanese ship was en route to a mission in foreign seas. The captain of the ship felt tired and thought of taking a bath. He went for taking the shower and removed his diamond ring and Rolex and kept them on the table.

When he returned after taking the bath, he found that the ring and watch were stolen.

He called the five members of the crew whom he suspected and asked them what they were doing for the last 15 minutes.

The Italian cook (with a butcher knife in hand): I was in fridge room getting meat for cooking.

The British Engineer (with a high beam torch in hand): I was working on generator engine.

The Pakistani seaman: I was on the mast correcting the flag which was upside down by mistake.

The Indian Radio officer: I was trying to make a contact with the company to inform them about our position.

The American navigation officer: I am on night watch, so I was sleeping in my cabin.

Upon listening to them, the captain caught the lying member.

Who do you think stole the valuables?

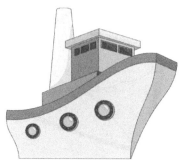

50

52. Suspicius Man

A girl was sitting in her hotel room when she heard a knock on the door. She opened the door and found that a man was standing outside.

The man said, "Oh! I am really sorry, I thought this was my room."

He then walked through the corridor to the elevator.

The girl did not know the man. She closed her door and called the security asking them to apprehend the man.

What made her suspicious of that man? He might have been genuinely mistaken.

53. Passcode Mystery Problem

While trying to pull out a robbery, a criminal came across a password lock. He has the following information with him that can assist him in cracking the password.Can you help him out?

1. The password is a 5-digit number.

2. The 4th digit is 4 more than the 2nd one.

3. The 3rd digit is 3 less than the 2nd one.

4. The 1st digit is three times the 5th digit.

5. Three pairs of digits sum up to 11.

54. Who Is The Killer?

A murder took place on the Baker Street. The murderer seemed a fan of Sherlock Holmes evident with the notes he/she left behind at the house at different locations.

When Sherlock Holmes arrived, he found out that the victim was a lady named Martha. She was shot and there were five suspects:
- Ben
- Lisa
- Catherine
- Marcus
- Phil

The notes that were left by the murderer were placed at different places and had a little description on them:

- The first note was found in the compound.

- The second note was found in the art room.

- The third note was found in the restroom.

- The fourth note was found in the underwater room.

- The fifth note was found in the smoking lounge.

- The sixth note was found in the makeup room.

All the notes had only one thing written on them:

"The clues are where you find the notes."

On examination, nothing was found anywhere.

Can you help Sherlock to decipher this puzzle?

55. Lateral Thinking Murder Or Suicide Riddle

Alexis jumped off the top of building a suicide attempt not knowing that a safety net is already there near the 8th floor. However, he was interrupted by a bullet shot at the back of head fired near the 10th story window.

Alexis falls on the safety net but was dead at the instance.

Normally if a person intends to commit suicide and his actions cause his death, it is a suicide even if the death does not take place in the way the person expected.

But if it's not the bullet Alexis must have survived.

Later on, investigation police found out that an old man angrily fired at her wife in the 1oth floor flat. however, shot missed the wife and hit the Alexis.

Normally, when a person intends to kill one human being and by his action kills another human being accidental, the charge is murder.

Later on the investigation, it was found out that gun was always unloaded and the man is just threatening his wife.

Further investigation revealed that the shotgun had been loaded by the couple's adult son, who was angry at his mother for cutting off monetary support. The son was hoping one day his father accidentally killed his mother.

Normally when a person plans something whose action kills another human being, the charge is murder.

Is this a murder or suicide and if murder who is guilty?

56. Logic Puzzle

A cat, a dog and a moneky were stolen. 3 suspects got caught: Harish, Manoj and Tarun.

All we know that each person stole one animal, but we do not know who stole which. Here are the investigation statements.

- Harish said: Tarun stole the cat.

- Manoj said: Tarun stole the dog.

- Tarun said: They both were lying. I did not steal the cat or the dog.

Later on, the police found out the man who stole the moneky told a lie.

The man who stole the cat told the truth.

Can you find out who stole which?

57. Detective Brain Teaser

Detective Ixolite of the NYPD was investigating a murder at Chicago.

It was a difficult case, and Ixolite was completely stumped until he noticed a message sent to him by the killer cunningly hidden in a newspaper advertisement selling Car Licence Plates.

Detective Ixolite thought about it for a while, and when he had solved the puzzle, immediately arrested the guilty man.

Q1) How did Ixolite know the advert was a clue for him?

Q2) Solve the code and tell me who Ixolite arrested.

This is the newspaper advert (Car licence plates for sale) that Detective Ixolite saw.

Plates For Sale;

- [W 05 NWO]
- [H 13 HSR]
- [O 05 EBM]
- [D 08 UNE]
- [U 10 HTY]
- [N 04 BRE]
- [N 16 TTE]
- [I 26 LHC]
- [T 10 AEE]
- [I 26 CNA]
- [X 22 VDA]

58. The Poison

In a party, two friends ordered single malt whiskey on the rocks. One of them drank five of the same in the time when his friend was able to drink only one.

Immediately after, his friend died. However the other one was feeling completely normal.

Both the drinks were poisoned.

How did the guy who drink five glasses survived?

59. Detective Question

A murder has been committed in a house. You are a detective and have to find out the murderer.

You investigate by asking three questions to each of the six suspects. Out of those six suspects, four are liars. It is not necessary that they speak everything a lie. But in their answers, there must be at least one lie. One of the six is the murderer.

There are eight rooms in the house in which the murder has been committed: Kitchen, Living Room, Bathroom, Garage, Basement, 3 Bedrooms.

At the time of the murder, only the murderer was present in the killing room. Any number of people can be present in any of the other rooms at the same time.

Can you identify the murderer and the four liars? Also can you find out who was in which room?

The responses of all the suspects are mentioned below.

Joseph:Peter was in the 2nd bedroom. So was I. David was in the bathroom.

Mandy: I agree with Joseph that David was in the bathroom and Peter was in the 2nd bedroom. But I think that Joseph was in the living room, OH MY GOD!

Peter: Mandy was in the kitchen with Christopher. But I was in the bathroom.

David: I still say Peter was in the 2nd bedroom and Jennifer was in the bathroom. Joseph was in the 1st bedroom.

Jennifer: Peter was in the bathroom with Christopher. And Mandy was in the kitchen.

Christopher: David was in the kitchen. And I was in the 2nd bedroom with Peter.

PS: The corpse was found in the Living Room.

60. House Party

A person was killed in a house party. When police arrives, there are six people present in the house who are the friends of the victim.

The name of the friends are:
- Rohit,
- Aman,
- Nick,
- Gagan,
- Randy.

Near the dead body, they find a few numbers written with blood by the victim on floor.

The numbers are 8, 5, 4 and 11.

The police arrests one of the friends for the murder.

Whom did they arrest and why?

61. Who Killed Billy?

Billy "The Knife," the infamous tough guy, was found murdered one night in an alleyway behind the nightclub he used to frequently visit. The police brought in three suspects on the next morning. One of the officers interrogated the three men and noted down the following statements.

Alex:
1. I did not kill Billy.
2. Jimmy is not my friend.
3. I knew Billy.

Jimmy:
1. I did not kill Billy.
2. Alex and Dexter are friends of mine.
3. Alex did not kill Billy.

Dexter:
1. I did not kill Billy.
2. Alex lied when he said that Jimmy was not his friend.
3. I do not know who killed Billy.

Only one of the three is guilty, and only one of each man statements is false.

Who killed Billy the Knife ?

62. Sherlock Holmes Murderer Puzzle

The fifth richest man in the Baker Street named Mr. Bill Richman is kidnapped. Sherlock Holmes is appointed on the case. At the crime scene, a note is found written by Mr. Richman. The note read:

"First of January, Fourth of October, Fifth of March, Third of June."

Sherlock knew that somehow, the killer name was hidden in the note. The following were the suspects:

- Jack Richman, the son and the heir of property.

- John Jacobson, the employee of Richman.

- June Richman, the wife of Richman.

Sherlock took only a few moments to deduce the killer name.

Can you tell who was the killer?

63. Chelsea Hacker

Chelsea football website was hacked by one of the players. Jose, the coach of Chelsea has shortlisted five players as the possible hacker.

Each suspected player made three statements from each suspected player and out of which two are true and one is false.

Terry:
A) I have not hacked the website.
B) I know nothing about hacking.
C) Costa did it.

Hazard:
A) I have not hacked the website.
B) The website was attacked by one of the players.
C) I hate Shelly

Remy:
A) I have not hacked the website.
B) I have never seen Oscar in my entire life.
C) I am sure Costa did it.

Costa:
A) I have not hacked the website.
B) I am sure Oscar did it.
C) Terry was lying when he said he did it.

Oscar:
A) I have not hacked the website.
B) I am sure Hazard did it.
C) I used to be friend with Remy.

So who hacked the website?

64. L Lawliet Chemist Murder Mystery

To attend world science seminar, a famous chemist from Russia visit Tokyo (Japan). In the lab, the scientist was killed and his six assistants were under suspicion of killing the chemist.

Name of six assistants:
- Austin,
- Wayne,
- Dege,
- Oscaru,
- Lingard,
- Rojo.

He left a note:

"76-20-44 79-16-22-7"

A local detective L Lawliet was called to solve the case.

After reading the note, L Lawliet instantly asked the police to arrest the murderers.

Who are the murderers?

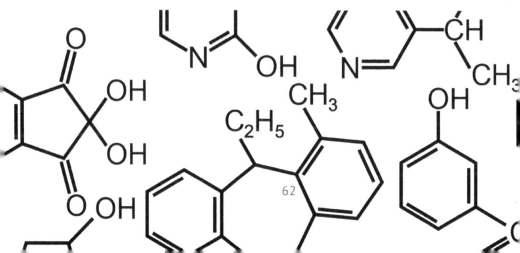

65. Bank Thieves Brain Teaser

The BlahBlah bank of London is abducted by the robbers. The head of the robbers asked the cashier to empty their money vault to them and when suddenly cashier got a call from her father.

To avoid any suspicion, the robber asked the cashier to pick the call and reply her father in the shortest manner possible.

The cashier told her father "Is there an emergency father, Call me when you are free and I will help you in your furnishing" and then the cashier hung up the phone.

After 10 minutes, police arrived at the crime scene.

How did the police know about the robbery?

Solutions

1. **The Murdering Type** - Max's agent, Roger, was arrested. Detective Sing had looked at Max's last written message again and discovered that the columnist had typed out the identity of his murderer, but his fingers had been one line up on the keys from where they should have been. Instead of writing "Roger stabbed me," he had written "49t34 w5qgg3e j3."

2. **'Murder,' Quoth The Bible** - The detective arrested Sean's brother, John. He deduced that Sean had suspected his brother of being jealous of him and his business and written the note to point the authorities in his brother's direction in case anything happened to him.The first clue was the passage, "Seek Him if you want to know why I did leave you," which pointed the detective towards the Bible. He then surmised that "4:10" might actually be referring to a specific Bible passage and not a time, and that "AM" might be referring to the Old Testament. He then needed to know which book of the Bible to check and deduced that "Jenna, Sis" might refer to the book of Genesis. When he checked the passage, he found that it was the story of the very first murder, in which Cain killed his brother Abel out of jealousy.

3. **Jumping To Conclusions** - If the person had taken their own life, one of the windows would have been open, but they were all closed.

4. **Stone Cold Killer** - Adrian's body was still wearing mittens when he was found, so he could not have left fingerprints on the rock that James claimed killed Lulo. They concluded that James must have ended them both and planted Adrian's fingerprints to cover his tracks.

5. **Sound The Alarm** - Edward set a tray on the edge of a table. He placed heavy pans on one side and counterbalanced them with blocks of ice on the other. When the ice eventually melted after several hours, the weight of the pans sent the tray crashing to the floor, tripping the alarm. The police had initially dismissed the pans, tray, and puddle of water as simply more clutter from the ransacking.

6. **Special Delivery** - The newspaper delivery person was arrested for the crime. They hadn't delivered Tuesday's or Wednesday's newspapers because they knew the wealthy man was already dead by their hand.

7. **Kidnapped Kid** - This is a true story from Taiwan.
When the rich man reached the phone booth he found a carrier pigeon in a cage. It had a message attached telling the man to put the diamond in a small bag which was around the pigeon's neck and to release the bird. When the man did this the police were powerless to follow the bird as it returned across the city to its owner.

8. **Self-Inflicted Gunshot Wound** - Because Aiers's shirt was only marred by the hole and a small bloodstain, the gun barrel must have been some distance away from his body. Being a little person, Aiers's arms were not long enough to have held the gun far enough away from his body to shoot himself without leaving gunshot residue.

9. **Mystery of the Ancient Temple** - The idols from left to right are: God of Diplomacy, God of Falsehood, God of Truth.
The God of Truth is not seated on the left because he always speaks the truth whereas the idol on the left replied that the God of Truth is seated at the centre.
The God of Truth is also not seated in the centre as he always speaks the truth but the idol at the centre replied that the God of Diplomacy is seated at the centre.
Therefore, the God of Truth is seated on the right. As God of Truth is seated on the right, and he always speaks the truth, then the The God of Falsehood is seated at the centre. The God of Diplomacy is seated on the left and he has lied.

10. **Detective Bethoven** - Strauss is the one who killed Handel. You need to take turns assuming someone is the killer; that means everyone's second sentence is a lie. If Joplin was the killer, Grieg's lie mixed with Strauss' counteracts the other. If Grieg was the killer, Gershwin would need to be a killer too. If Gershwin was the killer, Gershwin would need to be a killer too. If Gershwin was the killer, Grieg and Strauss counter each other again, but with Strauss, everything would fit in.

11. **Window Pain In The Neck** - Frost forms on the inside of windows when they are exposed to cold air outside and warm, humid air inside. The man could not have wiped frost off of the outside of the window pane.

12. **Love At First Funeral** - The young woman assumed that the young man was somehow connected to her family and that he might attend her sister's funeral like he did her mother's.

13. **The Cook, The Maid, Two Friends, And A Niece** - Detective Marshall was able to see the sun setting through the bay window during her interrogation, indicating that she was facing west; however, Mandy had stated that she had seen the sun rising through the same bay window when she had noticed her uncle's body.
Clearly, Mandy had been lying and was guilty of the crime.
Detective Marshall later surmised that Mandy had shot her uncle with a revolver hidden in the kitchen after learning he had disowned her and written her out of his will.

14. **Share And Share Alike** - The old woman coated one side of the knife with liquid cyanide. When she sliced the apple in half, only the young woman's portion was poisoned.

15. **Press Play For Murder** - If the man had actually recorded himself during the act, the detective would have had to rewind the tape to hear his message.

16. **Message In The Sand** - Considering the woman had crawled toward the water instead of away from it, and since she likely knew her time was short, the detective didn't believe she would have written "help," but instead the name of her attacker: "Shelby."
The detective theorized that the woman had discovered the club owner was cheaitng his employees and planned to finger him, so Shelby followed her out of the club and assailed her near the beach.

17. **No Alibis In Murder Mansion** - The maid was arrested, as the murder occured on a Sunday when there is no mail delivery.

18. **Loose Lips** - The maid had only told the man that his wife was hurt, not that she had been shot. He only could have known this if he was the one who shot her.

19. **Who Killed The Maya?** - The killer is Kylie because there was no alcohol left at the bar, so Kylie could not order a beer.

20. **Who Is Lying?** Jane's brother is lying because he said that Jane was depressed because she had fired from work. but her boss said he hadn't seen Jane in her office. So, the liar is Jane's brother.

21. **Who Killed His Wife?** - The killer is ROBERT. It was not a bank locker code. She encoded the murderer's name.

22. **The Stolen Bracelet** - Cathy was convicted of fraud because the bedroom window was broken from the inside. If somebody had broken in from the outside, there would have been glass pieces on the bedroom floor. Also, the room was perfectly tidy, which means the so-called thief didn't search for items and knew exactly where the bracelet was.

23. **The Old Woman Who Lived Alone** - The mailman killed the old woman because the newspapers for Wednesday and Thursday weren't found in or outside the house. This means he knew there would be no one to read them. (He tried to trick the police by reporting the crime himself - but turns out he isn't too smart at creating riddles after all)

24. **Deadly Chemicals** - The list of chemicals had a clue - their abbreviations spell out the murderer's name, Ni-C-O-La-S.

25. **Grand Theft Auto** - Consider that six statements are false. A's first statement and C's first statement contradict each other. One of them is false. C's and D's contradict each other. One of them is false. Therefore, there are four additional false statements. Assume A is guilty. If so, A's second statement, B's second statement, and D's first statement are the additional false statements. Assume D is guilty. If so, A's second statement, B's first statement, and D's third statement are false. This also only makes five false statements. D did not do it.Assume C did it. If so, A's second statement, D's first and third statements are false. This again, makes only five false statements. After ruling out suspects A, C and D, B is the culprit. B's third statement, C's second statement, and D's first and third statements are the additional false statements. This adds up to six.

26. **The Poison Murder** - The killer froze the poison turned it to ice. The victim putted ice cubes into his cup and then he took few of the ice cubes from the cup into his coke.Detective Thompson figured that because when the ice on both cups melted, the coke is 20% poison and the water is just poison in liquid form.

27. **Job Interview** - Because pages 165 and 166 of every book are on the same sheet of paper!

28. **The Diamond Robbery** - When Detective Thompson was outside, he saw the window, along with shattered pieces of glass under his feet. This meant that the glass was broken from inside. The keeper had gone to his mother's place, and the only person who had access to the inside of the house was Mr. Fred.

29. **Archeological Dig** - Detective Thompson realized that Bob had been taken in by the local native because there couldn't be any coins dated B.C. How would anyone have known it was B.C?

30. **The Burglary Job** - Joss is the gunman, Erick is the planner, Hewitt is the lookout, and Cooper is the innocent bystander. Fact 1: The gunner was in Edinburgh for the preceding week, so he wasn't Erick, Cooper or Hewitt, they were all somewhere not-in-Edinburgh some time in the week before, leaving Joss to be the gunman. Fact 2: Joss acquainted with Cooper (tennis), Cooper knows Erick (surveillance duty), and Erick acquainted with Hewitt (dinner). Inspector Baldwin said that the innocent bystander was acquainted with the planner and the gunman (Joss), but not with the lookout. That obviously states that Cooper is the innocent bystander. The rest is easy.

31. **The Dying Message** - It's Dr. Robert Green.Mrs. Bennet was grasping a yellow and blue pieces of paper. Mix blue and yellow, and we get green, that points to the doctor's last name. Detective Thompson also gives the argument to Inspector Lucas that Mrs. Bennet can't wrote the killer's name, as she knew that there's big chance that the doctor will be the first person to examine her body, thus he will have the opportunity to get rid of the "dying message". So, she had to leave something that isn't obvious, that the doctor won't realize it right away.

32. **Are You Mocking Me?** - It's Mark Jones. ? = question mark, so the clue reads "Question mark Jones. He broke your window."

33. **Thompson's Game** - The items made from synthetic materials (polyester, plastic, acrylic) all have something in them. The items made from natural materials (cotton, cardboard, paper) are all empty. Therefore the plastic bowl (being synthetic) has the chips and the wood bowl (being natural) is empty.

34. **Diamonds Are Forever** - The waiter put the diamonds in one of the glasses, blend them with ice. He intends to gather them later when no-one was around.Detective Thompson noticed this because there are 5 glasses on the table, while there are only 4 persons to served (Mr. Bronson and his three guests).

35. **Weak Hand** - Alex was previously bragged about baseball, so Thompson assumed that he's quite proficient with ball. A left handed baseball player is used to put his glove in his right hand to catch the ball and would use his strong hand (the left one) to throw the ball. Alex caught the trinket with his right hand only shows he's left-handed. A circumstantial evidence, but enough as a based for thorough interrogation.Note that although Davie dropped the trinket, it doesn't mean that he's left-handed, as Ian threw the trinket by surprise, it's impossible to purposely use his weak-hand to catch the ball. Different case for Alex, that although his right is the weak one, it has a good reflex as a result from playing baseball.

36. **Royal Riddle** - "Blue." At first, this problem seems to be impossible to solve. The only real clue that the Emperor gave is that there is at least one blue hat, which is useless since the women can clearly see that there are at least two blue hats. Now, we (as the winner lady did) have to work on an assumption: We already know that the three hats are not all white because the Emperor said at least one hat was blue. What if there were two white hats and one blue hat (which obviously isn't the case)? Then the wise woman with the blue hat would have seen two white hats and immediately called out that her own hat was blue, since she knew there weren't 3 white hats. Now the only real question is, "Are there two or three blue hats?" Consider this less obvious situation- that there were exactly two blue hats. This seems a very real possibility at first, after all, our lady can see exactly two blue hats. So everyone sits and thinks - for a little while. But if there are only two blue hats, then two people will see one blue and one white hat. These two people will very quickly, by virtue of the other's silence, rule out the possibility that there is only one blue hat. One of these two lucky women would cry blue within a few short minutes, if that long. There is only one case which forces the three women to sit in silence - three blue hats. However, our lady, through her sharp wits and bravery was the first to reach this conclusion.

37. **One Wish** - The servant said, "My mother wants to see her grandson swinging on a swing of gold."

38. **Sports Day** - 1st place is Janet (no. 4) wore red 2nd place is Jessica (no. 2) wore green 3rd place is Julie (no. 1) wore blue 4th places is Josie (no. 3) wore yellow - Julie wasn't wearing 2 and yellow (clue 3) so wasn't wearing green (clue 6). - Janet was wearing red (clue 1) and Josie wore yellow (clue 5), hence Julie wore blue, leaving Jessica wearing green, which also wearing 2 (clue 6). - As Jessica wore 2, she didn't come 3rd (clue 2), and Janet came first (clue 1), which means that Jessica must have come 2nd in order to beat the girl wearing 3 (clue 5). - We now know Janet won and Jessica was 2nd, therefore Julie must have come 3rd in order to beat the girl in yellow (clue 3), leaving Josie in last place. - As Jessica came second and she beat the girl wearing 3 (clue 5), the girl wearing 3 must have come 4th (therefore Josie) as the girl wearing 1 came 3rd (clue 2). Julie (who is 3rd) wore 1 (clue 2), leaving Janet wearing 4.

39. **Adventure Race** - First, Annie and Bob make the crossing (2 minutes), then Annie comes back (1 minute). Next, Charles crosses with Dan (10 minutes), and told Bob to takes the canoe back (2 minutes). Annie and Bob will make the last crossing (2 minutes), which gives the total of 2+1+10+2+2 = 17 minutes.

40. **Pennies** - Just pull one coin from the container labeled "MIXED" None of the container was labeled correctly, so this surely isn't the mixed container. Thus, if you pulled a 2005 penny, the container labeled "1975" must be the mixed container, and the one labeled "2005" is the 1975 container. This also goes the other way around.

41. **Bulbs** - Turn two of the light switches on. Wait a while, and then turn one of them off, then quickly enter the attic. One light will be on, one off, and one off but still hot.

42. **Farmer's Dilemma** - Take the goose over first and come back. Then take the fox over and bring the goose back. Now leave the goose and take the corn over. The corn should be safe with the fox, and come back alone to get the goose. Take the goose over and the job is done.

43. Great Pumpkin - The fastest way of turning all the lantern off are by 7 blows. How to do it is by blowing each lantern in order, like this:

- You blow lantern 1: 7 (off) - 1 (off) - 2 (off) - 3 (lit) - 4 (lit) - 5 (lit) - 6 (lit)
- You blow lantern 2: 7 (off) - 1 (lit) - 2 (lit) - 3 (off) - 4 (lit) - 5 (lit) - 6 (lit)
- You blow lantern 3: 7 (off) - 1 (lit) - 2 (off) - 3 (lit) - 4 (off) - 5 (lit) - 6 (lit)
- You blow lantern 4: 7 (off) - 1 (lit) - 2 (off) - 3 (off) - 4 (lit) - 5 (off) - 6 (lit)
- You blow lantern 5: 7 (off) - 1 (lit) - 2 (off) - 3 (off) - 4 (off) - 5 (lit) - 6 (off)
- You blow lantern 6: 7 (lit) - 1 (lit) - 2 (off) - 3 (off) - 4 (off) - 5 (off) - 6 (lit)
- You blow lantern 6: 7 (off) - 1 (off) - 2 (off) - 3 (off) - 4 (off) - 5 (off) - 6 (off)

Congratulations! The Great Pumpkin decides to save your soul, just this time though...

44. Smart Farmer - The farmer said: "I shall be hanged!" If the farmer was lying, he would be hanged. But that's what the farmer was saying. So he speaks the truth. But if he speaks the truth, he would be beheaded, so then he was not speaking the truth. So it is impossible for the judge to determine wether the farmer speaks the truth or not. So therefore the judge cannot determine the penalty and sets the farmer free.

45. Point To The Murderer - Jeff Killed Mike 1. Jack is not the murderer because he is the brother of the murderer. 2. Dan can't be the murderer since he ran a marathon, and the murderer recently had his leg amputated, and wouldn't be running a marathon of any magnitude that quickly. 3. Ben is not the murderer if he just met Jack since Jack and the murderer grew up together. 4. This leaves Jeff and Mike. Since Jeff is still alive (he wants to install a new computer next week, present tense) he must be the murderer. Mike also didn't grow up with Jack. It has been determined that Jack, Dan, and Jeff are all alive. Ben must also be alive since Jeff plans to install Ben computer next week. This means that Jeff killed Mike.

46. Detective Tip - Bill. If you read the message upside down, you'll notice that the numbers resemble letters and that those letters form legible sentences. The message is 'Bill is boss. He sells oil.'

47. **Who Is The Killer?** - Jason Negithe - number on the calendar was written in a hurry , police matched the written number with the months of the year. So the B was an 8, thereby giving us 7-8-9-10-11: July, August, September, October, November. Use the first letter of each month and it spells J-A-S-O-N.

48. **Murder Mystery Problem** - Mother. We know from (3) that the youngest person was not the victim, from (4) that the youngest person was not the helper and from (6) that the youngest person was not the killer. The youngest person can only have been the witness therefore. If we make up a chart there are now three possible combinations: Oldest person (father) H H MNext to oldest (mother) V M HNext to youngest (son) M V V Youngest (daughter) W W W(H = Helper ; V = Victim ; M = Murderer ; W = Witness) We can work out from (5) that the father was the oldest, from (2) that the youngest person must have been the daughter. Therefore the next to the youngest must have been the son and the next to the oldest, the mother. Of three possibilities: the first is impossible (from (3) - the youngest person and the victim were of different sexes); the third is also impossible (from (1) - the witness and the helper were of different sexes). Therefore only the second possibility holds - and the mother was the murderess.

49. **Elevator Puzzle** - The man is a of short stature. He can't reach the upper elevator buttons, but can push is with his umbrella.

50. **Crack The Code** - The code word is TIE. Suppose if you are told a character of MOD, then you can't identify if the number of vowels are one or two. Suppose that the character you are told of is M, then you can associate two words with it i.e. AIM (that has two vowels) and MOD (that has 1 vowel). You can say the same regarding other characters O and D as well. Thus all those words that comprises of M, O or D in them can be ruled out. This points us to TIE. If you check with the characters of TIE, you will agree that it stands true for each of the characters of the word. Thus this is the code word.

51. **Point To The Thief** - The Pakistani seaman is lying. This is because the Japanese flag looks the same upside down. There was no need to correct it and thus he is plainly lying.

52. **Suspicius Man** - The suspicion was natural. If the man thought the room was his, he would have tried the keys and not knocked on the door.

53. **Passcode Mystery Problem** - The 5-digit password is 65292.

54. **Who Is The Killer?** - While it may have sounded a bit too difficult, it is not that difficult to crack. The murderer is Marcus. The notes were found in the Compound, Art Room, Restroom, Underwater Room, Smoking Lounge and Makeup Room. Now, if we just look at the first letter of each, we will have - C, A, R, U, S and M. If you arrange the letters, you will get the name Marcus.

55. **Lateral Thinking Murder Or Suicide Riddle** - The death was ruled a suicide.

56. **Logic Puzzle** - Harish stole Moneky (R $ C) Tarun stole Dog (T $ D) Manoj stole Cat (S $ H).

57. **Detective Brain Teaser** - 1) The first bit is easy, as the first letter of each plate spells WHODUNNIT IX (A challenge to our Detective.) 2) The second bit is a little trickier, but I gave you the solution. If you read the last three letters in each plate from the bottom up and right to left you get ADVANCE EACH LETTER BY THE NUMBER SHOWN, so advance W by 5 to get B, H by 13 to get U and so on until you spell BUTLER DID IT.

58. **The Poison** - The guy who drank five glasses survived because the poison was in the middle of ice cubes. He drank rapidly and thus the ice had no chance to melt in his drink while the other one drank slowly and thus enough ice had melted in his drink to poison it heavily and he died.

59. **Detective Question** - Assume that Peter is not in the second bedroom. This suggests that Joseph, Mandy, David and Christopher are liars. This further suggests that Peter and Jennifer speak truth. But they cannot be as they do not correspond on Christopher's location. Hence we have assumed wrong and Peter is in second bedroom. By saying that, we have established that Peter is in the second bedroom. Also, Peter and Jennifer are liars. Assume that Joseph speaks truth. This suggests that David is in the bathroom and Joseph in the second bedroom. This further suggests Mandy and David are liars as they told that Joseph was not in the second bedroom. Also suggests that Christopher lied, as he said David is in kitchen. Therefore, there are three new liars, totaling 5 liars, which is a contradiction given the situation in the question. Thus, we have established that Joseph is a liar. Assume that Mandy speaks truth. This suggests that Joseph was in the living room and David in the Kitchen.

This further suggests that David and Christopher are liars. But again, this contradicts as we have concluded that there are again 5 liars (including above 3 established liars). Thus, we have established that Mandy is a liar. David and Christopher speak truth. Jennifer was in the bathroom. Joseph was in the first bedroom. David was in the kitchen. Christopher was in second bedroom with Peter. The killer has to be Mandy as no one else was present in the living room.

60. **House Party** - The police arrested Aman. This is because the numbers corresponds to the months. 8 - August 5 - May 4 - April 11 - November. Now taking the initials of the months, Aman is the name the victim was trying to tell.

61. **Who Killed Billy?** - Jimmy. It is not Alex because if it was, Alex 1 and Jimmy 3 would both be false, which would make Alex 2 and Jimmy 2 both true which is a contradiction. It is not Dexter because if it was, Dexter 1 and Dexter 3 would both be false, which is not possible. Therefore, it must be Jimmy.

62. **Sherlock Holmes Murderer Puzzle** - The kidnapper was John Jacobson. All you have to do is read the note carefully. First of January = First letter of January i.e. J. Similarly, octOber, marcH, juNe. The name is JOHN.

63. **Chelsea Hacker** - Hazard

64. **L Lawliet Chemist Murder Mystery** - Oscaru and Austin. Explanation: The Chemist hide the name using periodic table as shown in below picture 76-20-44 => Os(76) + Ca(20) + Ru(44)79-16-22-7=> Au(79) + S(16) + Ti(22) + N(7)

65. **Bank Thieves Brain Teaser** - On phone, using pause button, the cashier messaged to her father "Emergency father, call help". Explanation: all Except one in bold is paused by the cashier."Is there an **emergency father, Call** me when you are free and I will **help** you in your furnishing"

Made in the USA
Las Vegas, NV
01 April 2021